MARKET HARBOROUGH & AROUND

THROUGH TIME

Stephen Butt

AMBERLEY PUBLISHING

First published 2013

Amberley Publishing
The Hill, Stroud, Gloucestershire, GL5 4EP
www.amberley-books.com

Copyright © Stephen Butt, 2013

The right of Stephen Butt to be identified as the
Author of this work has been asserted in accordance with
the Copyrights, Designs and Patents Act 1988.

ISBN 978 1 4456 1523 3 (print)
ISBN 978 1 4456 1546 2 (ebook)

British Library Cataloguing in Publication Data.
A catalogue record for this book is available from the
British Library.

Typesetting by Amberley Publishing.
Printed in Great Britain.

Contents

Introduction

Change is synonymous with the technological world of the twenty-first century and no town in England is immune from the effects of change. Familiar high street names are disappearing, and so too are many of the distinctive independent shops whose founders and their families have had roots in a certain town or village, sometimes for centuries.

Market Harborough was created as a place for trading, and its location was dictated by the construction of a highway connecting Oxendon in Northamptonshire with Kibworth in Leicestershire, which later extended to the county towns of Northampton and Leicester. In a sense, the town was designed to be a sort of 'service station' on this highway, close to the county boundary, where travellers could rest or stay overnight, purchase food and other goods, and where ancillary trades and professions such as blacksmiths and wheelwrights would have employment.

In the words of the architectural historian Nikolaus Pevsner, it is a 'created town, created by Henry II to be a market'. It became a manor in its own right in 1180. Before that time, the principal settlements in the area were Great Bowden, Little Bowden and Arden, all within walking distance of each other, and all of Anglo-Saxon origin. Market Harborough chapel is first mentioned around 1220, when it was dependent upon St Mary in Arden, itself a chapel of Great Bowden. Indeed, although a fine church, dedicated to St Dionysius, was constructed on the highway through the 'new' town, the church of St Mary in Arden, which survives today only as picturesque and rather poignant ruins, retained parish church status. It is for this reason that there is no churchyard attached to St Dionysius, since it started as a chapel of ease to Great Bowden.

Harborough probably derives from the Anglo-Saxon *haefera-beorg* meaning 'Oat Hill'. The market was operating by 1204 and has been held on Tuesdays, since 1221, without a break, though the traders now sell their wares inside a purpose-built market hall. The original market square remains, as does the High Street, though over the centuries it has been narrowed by buildings that gradually encroached upon the open space.

There is a small group of significant buildings that have stood overlooking the market and the High Street for centuries, and which epitomise an English market town. The magnificent broach spire of the parish church still dominates and despite the Victorian factories nearby, it has never been overshadowed. On the opposite side of the street is the Three Swans, one of several coaching inns that prospered in the town.

Naseby

In 1645 the people of Market Harborough found themselves at the very forefront of the bitter struggle of the English Civil Wars. With Oliver Cromwell and the Parliamentary army camped at Naseby, some 7 miles south of the town in Northamptonshire, Market Harborough became the headquarters for the Royalists. On 5 June, Charles I established his forces in the town, and on 13 June the Royalist army was quartered in the town, although the King himself probably stayed elsewhere, possibly in the manor of a loyal Royalist in the Leicestershire countryside nearby.

The battle of Naseby took place on the following day and was a decisive victory for Cromwell who led his troops. The defeated King's forces fled back across the Leicestershire border pursued by the the victorious Parliamentarians who lodged in Market Harborough overnight. The parish church was commandeered as a temporary prison camp. Cromwell wrote a letter to the Speaker of the House of Commons from Haverbrown, on 14 June, advising him of the victory.

Road, Rail and Canal

Although Market Harborough was created to serve people who travelled by road, the railways and the canals have also had a significant effect on the town. Market Harborough became connected to the canal network in the early years of the nineteenth century, at a time when the individual canal companies were building extensions to connect with each other. The Leicestershire & Northampton Union Canal had reached the village of Debdale, less than 5 miles north of Market Harborough, by 1797, but the company had run out of finance. By 1809, the canal had been completed as far as Market Harborough, but the continuation south towards the Grand Union Canal was halted due to lack of funds. The 5½-mile stretch of the canal from the Union Wharf just outside the town to the locks at Foxton is now known as the Grand Union Canal (Leicester Section–Market Harborough Branch).

It required considerable further investment and several years of major engineering projects to extend the network south from Foxton into Northamptonshire, including the construction of the locks and two long tunnels, and the terrain demanded that the canal took a long, meandering route. The Market Harborough branch also meanders, crossing the main A6 route between Market Harborough and Leicester.

The wharf at Market Harborough is located adjacent to the main road and became a distribution centre for coal and corn. In recent years it has attracted considerable investment, which has resulted in the sensitive refurbishment of the former canal buildings and the construction of waterside apartments. Today, the wharf is an attractive residential area, a tourist attraction and a safe mooring for canal boats.

The canal companies and the Victorian entrepreneurs who invested in them enjoyed only a relatively brief time of prosperity. The stair of locks at Foxton and the route south to Northampton was open fully by 1814, but only twenty-five years later the canals in the Midlands faced new competition from the London & Birmingham Railway.

The first railway station in Market Harborough was built in 1850 by the London & North Western Railway on its route from Stamford to Rugby and then south to Euston. In 1857, the Midland Railway extended its route from Leicester south through Bedford to London St Pancras, and later constructed a new joint station, which opened in 1885. Although the old LNWR line closed in 1966, resulting in the demolition of the platforms and, later, the viaduct over the Rockingham Road, the station building was retained and was successfully restored and refurbished in 1981.

Thomas Cook

The railways signalled the end of the commercial life of the canals and also had a devastating effect on the old stagecoach routes; but in Market Harborough, a young man saw the potential of the railways to effect beneficial social change. Thomas Cook was born in Melbourne in Derbyshire, but by the time he reached adulthood was travelling around the villages of Rutland, Northamptonshire and Lincolnshire as an itinerant Baptist preacher. Lack of money forced him to return to his former trade as a woodturner and he settled in Barrowden in Rutland where he met and married the daughter of a local farmer (and a Sunday school teacher) Marianne Mason.

They moved to Market Harborough where they met a local Baptist minister, Francis Beardsall, who was a strong supporter of the new temperance movement. Thomas joined up and was clearly strongly influenced by Beardsall's preaching. Within a short time, and despite the arrival of their only son John Mason Cook, he and Marianne began taking in temperance lodgers and writing and publishing magazines advocating temperance.

It was while Cook was on his way to Leicester along the old turnpike that he had his great idea. On 9 June 1841 Thomas Cook set out from his home in Market Harborough to attend a temperance meeting in the town of Leicester, some 15 miles away. About halfway along this road, he later wrote, 'a thought flashed through my brain – what a glorious thing it would be if the newly-developed powers of railways and locomotion could be made subservient to the promotion of temperance!' Thomas carried this idea with him to Leicester, where he suggested that a special train be engaged to carry the temperance supporters of the town to a meeting in Loughborough about four weeks later. The proposal was received with such enthusiasm that, on the following day, Thomas submitted his idea to the secretary of the Midland Railway Company. A train was subsequently arranged, and on 5 July 1841 around 500 passengers were conveyed in open carriages the enormous distance of 12 miles and back for a shilling. The day was a great success and, as Thomas later recorded, 'thus was struck the keynote of my excursions, and the social idea grew upon me'.

This was the beginning of Thomas Cook's venture into the travel world. His aim was to combine improvement with pleasure and to promote widely, through this 'business of travel', the causes in which he believed. Thomas continued travelling until the late 1880s, yet in all this time he shed none of his ideals. He succeeded in making travel easier, cheaper and safer for everyone, and his system of tours and excursions was described by W. E. Gladstone in 1887 as 'one of the humanising contrivances of the age'.

Thomas died on 18 July 1892, at the age of eighty-three, but his most famous legacy, the company that bears his name, continues to serve the travelling public today, more than 170 years after that first journey from Leicester to Loughborough.

The Symington Family

Around 1831 William Symington, a young Scotsman who had been selling tea and coffee in Harborough, acquired premises south of the Chain Bridge. He seems at first to have been chiefly a tea wholesaler, but in time his business became a large food preparing concern. The most important development, however, was the creation by James Symington, William Symington's brother, of a stay-making business. James Symington first came to Harborough in 1830 and established himself as a tailor and draper, but before long he became, in association with his wife, a stay-maker. The business was at first small, and it was not until 1850 that Symington first leased a building as a workshop. The introduction of Singer sewing machines in 1856 led to expansion. Around 1861 part of the former carpet factory was purchased, and in these premises, making great use of outworkers, James Symington and his sons built up the manufacture of corsets for the wholesale trade. The rest of the carpet factory was bought in 1876, and in 1884 a large new factory was built. This building, with its subsequent additions, still dominated the centre of Harborough in 1957.

CHAPTER 1

The Town
The High Street & The Square

At the heart of Market Harborough is the Square, originally the town's sheep market, and the once-broad High Street extending to the north. The spacious formality of the High Street can still be seen in the stretch of road from the old town hall to the boundary wall of Brooke House on the Leicester Road, but in the centre of the town encroachments and traffic management has changed the vista.

Despite the centuries of change and development, however, the atmosphere and character of this area is still dominated by four distinctive buildings whose own architectural histories span more than 600 years. Each of these buildings is still in use, and each represents an important facet of town life.

The magnificent broach spire of the parish church is regarded as one of the finest in England, and stands high above one corner of the Square. It is still the focal point of the town. In over 700 years, no other building nearby has challenged its supremacy. It has never been overshadowed, not even by the Victorian and Edwardian factories that were constructed close by.

On the opposite side of the High Street is the Three Swans, the best-known of several coaching inns that were once all prosperous in the town. In keeping with the typical layout of such buildings, the inn has a long, narrow yard behind its High Street frontage, which is accessed through an archway from the street, and a narrow extension of rooms that were formerly the stables. Once known simply as 'The Swan', this old inn is mentioned as early as 1517, and it is likely that at least a part of the frontage is almost that old.

Also in the shadow of the church spire is the old grammar school, established by a local man, Robert Smyth, who, unlike Dick Whittington, from humble beginnings found fame and fortune in London. It is said that Smyth (or Smith) walked to London from Market Harborough in about 1570, and thirty years later was the comptroller of the City of London. In 1607 he returned to his birthplace and founded a grammar school, a fascinating building built on wooden 'stilts', either to separate the pupils from the sheep and other animals at the market beneath, or to give the market traders some measure of protection from the elements. This building, so full of character still, gives shelter to traders in the twenty-first century.

At the northern end of the street stands the impressive old town hall that was built in 1788 and now forms a distinctive 'gateway' to the High Street at the junction of Abbey Street and Church Street. The building also marks part of the intrusion into the original spacious square. As in Leicester and in Leicestershire's other market towns, certain traders became so established, and possibly so dominant in the community, that

their once-temporary stalls were replaced by permanent structures of bricks and mortar. In the case of Market Harborough an entire new street, Church Street, was formed.

The Square and the High Street are still busy and bustling, but the shoppers and tourists have to compete with the ever-present road traffic, including heavy goods vehicles. Despite a bypass to the east of the town, the High Street is still used daily by thousands of vehicles travelling through Market Harborough to the motorways and major trunk roads.

The High Street

The nineteenth-century photographer George Henton makes clever use of the group of children to provide a sense of scale in his view of High Street looking towards the Square. The old town hall, built in 1788, still dominates this approach to the town from the south, as does the distinctive spire of the parish church of St Dionysius.

The High Street from the Square

The present High Street seems somewhat sanitised when compared with the business and 'busyness' of the earlier photograph. In the place of the sign for The Hind, one of the town's old coaching inns, is one for the modern Wildwood Restaurant.

The Parish Church and the Three Swans
Two important elements of town life: the church
and the inn, connected in another photograph
by George Henton of Leicester, who was an
artist of note as well as a fine photographer.

The Parish Church

In the earlier photograph, the car provides a good indication of the height of the spire. In the words of Nikolaus Pevsner, it is 'elegant yet dignified, refined and in no way excessive'.

The Parish Church Sundial

The sundial on the south side of the tower of the parish church of St Dionysius dates to the early eighteenth century. It was restored in 1948. The message to the shoppers who pass by is 'Improve the Time'.

The Three Swans and High Street

The High Street looking north. The Three Swans was one of five coaching inns in the town (the others being The Hind, The Peacock, The Angel and The Talbot). Originally known as The Swanne, it changed its name in 1790 – possibly because the original sign that had just one Swan gained two more in 1780.

The Old Grammar School

This building in neat, quaint Tudor style was built in 1614 as a gift to the town from local man Robert Smyth, who had made his fortune in London. The bell cote was added in 1789. In addition to providing a schoolroom on the first floor, it has for centuries protected traders beneath from inclement weather.

The Market Square

This is a rare early photograph by one of the earliest female professional photographers in Leicestershire, Susan Jennings. She probably took this picture from her studios above the street. The long exposure has caused blurring of moving figures. The Talbot Inn became the Market Tavern and is now a pizza and pasta restaurant. The market, held here since 1219, was moved to an indoor hall in 1992.

The Square

Compared with the previous image, this photograph taken in the 1930s is of a more elegant scene that almost denies its heritage. The Square is now an area for parking motor vehicles, and there are well-kept flower borders. The long shadows and the extended shop canopies suggest late afternoon on a summer's day.

The Square, 1836

The artist provides a very wide perspective and a view that possibly never existed in reality. The lone rider and horse, and the factory chimney on the skyline, add to the feeling that this is a view of a vanishing world. Today there is little sense of spaciousness in this busy location.

High Street Parade, 1968
The location for this ceremonial march past by the cadets of the local Air Training Corps is the northern section of High Street. Joules, which occupies the shop on the right of the photographs, is a local business that has traded in the town for many years.

No. 19 High Street

Mr W. H. Stevens owned and managed one of the earliest garages in the town. In this photograph from 1906 he is standing in the doorway, and in the car is his apprentice Ernest Allen, who later opened a garage in Great Bowden. The original building, which was probably built in the sixteenth century, was demolished in the 1920s. Later, this was the location of Woolworths before that store moved to Nos 43–45 The Square. The adjacent building was the Stamford, Spalding & Boston Bank and still serves that purpose.

The Old Town Hall

Originally used as a market hall and butchers' shambles, the old town hall was built in 1788, probably by the Earl of Harborough 'partly for the tammy manufacturers'. The Earl's arms are set into the elevation facing the High Street. 'Tammy' was a fine worsted, production of which was at its height in the town in the latter half of the eighteenth century.

Church Street from Church Square

Church Street, also known as Church Gate, was formed by the construction of buildings encroaching on the eastern side of the formerly wide High Street. Narrow and winding, it has a distinctive character of its own and is now the location of a variety of independent shops and boutiques.

Church Square Looking South
The building that now houses the lively Harborough Theatre was once the Green Dragon Inn. Sections of the structure date to the seventeenth century.

Church Square Looking East

This is where the architecture of industry meets the earlier structures of the market and High Street. This photograph from around 1914 shows the two Symington factory buildings towering above the diminutive Dolphin Inn, which was demolished in 1936 to make way for a factory extension.

The Square in Spring Snow
Climate change and unseasonal weather became news headlines when a snowstorm hit Market Harborough in May 1951.

The Square

The parade took place in November 1975. The road has now vanished as part of the landscaping of this important central area of the town. The supermarket, built in the 1960s, is architecturally incongruous in this sensitive setting.

The Square: Traffic in 1951

Despite the continuation of rationing, the *Market Harborough Advertiser and Midland Mail* reported on the problems of traffic in the Square and High Street, and hoped that one day a purpose-built bus station would put an end to the traffic jams and indiscriminate parking.

Leicester Road from Brooke House
The 'gateway' to Market Harborough on the Leicester Road from the south. The arches of the old town hall can be seen in the distance. The retaining wall is the boundary of Brooke House.

CHAPTER 2

The Town
Streets & Structures

In the eighteenth century, Market Harborough was described as consisting of three streets and four lanes. These were, presumably, High Street, Church Street and Adam and Eve Street, which form a triangle with the parish church at its centre. The aforementioned lanes probably included Bowden Lane, St Mary's Lane and Lubbenham Lane (now Coventry Road).

Together with the main turnpike from Northampton to Leicester, these lanes and streets formed the nucleus of what had been until that time a market town at the heart of a wider rural community. The next stage of road building was to be prompted by the growth of industry and the consequent influx of workers from the surrounding villages. Abbey Street was built in 1901, creating a junction in the centre of the High Street, immediately opposite the old town hall, and cutting through the site of the former Coach & Horses inn. In 1936, Roman Way was created, leaving the centre of the town near to the east end of the parish church and cutting through an earlier network of small houses and cottages.

The outward development is where the various municipal buildings can be found, including the fire station and ambulance station, almost opposite each other in Abbey Street, the Nonconformist churches, the gasworks, and the railway station, the latter being closer to the centre of Little Bowden than that of Market Harborough.

Historically, the River Welland has been a significant topographical landmark, the last river to cross before travellers from the north entered Northamptonshire. A bridge was in place by 1228, and by 1675 it was a structure of considerable size with six arches. Its length was possibly due to the meandering nature of the river, which changed course at least once and often flooded the surrounding low-lying land. From as early as 1615 it was decreed that vehicles could use the bridge only when the ford was impassable. A chain was placed across the bridge at all other times, which gave the bridge the name of the 'Chain Bridge'. The main road was turnpiked by 1750, which prompted a major rebuilding of the bridge in 1746. As road traffic increased, the bridge was again replaced, in 1814 and most recently in 1928.

The river has now been tamed and is part of the retail landscape of the St Mary's shopping centre as well as the scenery of Welland Park, but the centre of Market Harborough is still subject to flooding despite several recent flood prevention schemes.

Abbey Street

The town's fire station was constructed in 1903 and extended ten years later to a matching design by Coales and Johnson. The first two bays are the original building. The two adjoining houses were built by the same company in 1912 to provide homes for firemen.

Ambulance Station

The original architect's design of 1923 for the town's quaint ambulance station in Abbey Street. Today, the building is used by St John Ambulance. As it is located almost directly opposite the fire station, there must have been considerable excitement when both services were called out at the same time.

Coventry Road Towards High Street
The Symington factory can be seen looming in the distance in this photograph from around 1935. In the centre is the Bell Inn, selling wines and spirits from the local brewery, Eady & Dulley's.

Coventry Road

This was formerly known as Lubbenham Lane, which is probably a more accurate indication of the route that this street leads to. The Catholic church of Our Lady of Victories stands at the junction with Fairfield Road.

Symington & Thwaites

Standing on the corner of Adam and Eve Street and St Mary's Road, this grocery business was started by Walter Symington, a nephew of William Symington who founded the family's first manufacturing business in the town. The business moved here from smaller premises a few doors away and continued trading until 1960. Coffee is a beverage from Symington's time that is still sold here.

Brooklands

A sedate house on the Northampton Road, and close to the bridge over the River Welland, Brooklands served as the local government headquarters before the acquisition of the Symington building in Adam and Eve Street. Even earlier, the Urban District Council offices were also on Northampton Road, on the opposite side of the street.

Northampton Road
South of the river, and past the former brewery site where the modern bus station and covered market now stand, the old route to Northampton is now principally the axis of a residential area constructed mainly since the Second World War.

The Peacock Hotel, *c.* 1879–99
Despite its prime location at one of the busiest road junctions in the centre of the town, the future of The Peacock was in doubt until taken over by an international fast-food chain. The building has also been given new life by being incorporated into the St Mary's shopping centre.

Nos 88–93 St Mary's Road

These sedate houses were typical of the appealing mix of architectural styles that once gave a sense of character to St Mary's Road. The most recent of residential apartments are an improvement architecturally on earlier and less-controlled development.

St Mary's Road

Residential apartments, nearing completion in March 2013, stand on the site of the earlier Georgian and Victorian houses. The parade is taking place here because the building in the centre of the photograph was the first headquarters of 1084 Squadron (Market Harborough) Air Training Corps.

St Mary's Road Towards the Square
A delightful mix of different buildings, looking along the northern side of St Mary's Road towards the town centre from the junction with Mill Hill Lane. The early photograph dates to around 1878.

Cattle Market and Settling Rooms
The square tower of the Settling Rooms can be seen above the pigpens of the former cattle market. The building has been refurbished and is now the focal point of the car park serving the St Mary's shopping centre.

Air Training Corp Headquarters

Next to the pens in which sheep were kept prior to auction stood the ATC Squadron hut, which was demolished to make way for the St Mary's shopping centre car park. The River Welland marks the northern boundary of the car park, and a commemorative landscaped walk was laid out to mark the Millennium.

Lathkill Street

Other roads nearby have maintained their original character, but business development on the edge of the town has changed much of Lathkill Street beyond recognition.

The Harborough Rubber Company, St Mary's Road

Originally John Bland's steam-driven flour mill, built around 1860, the Harborough Rubber Company acquired these buildings in 1894, producing pedal blocks for bicycles and cars, and later more precision-designed parts for aircraft. The company adopted the brand name 'Dainite' during the First World War when the factory was in production throughout the day and night. The engine house is a listed building and stands next to modern apartments.

The Railway Station

The stationmaster, his staff and possibly his children line up outside the attractive London & North Western Railway station built in 1850. This present station, constructed nearby, was opened in 1885 to serve the Midland Railway and the LNWR. Although the old LNWR route is no more, the building has been carefully renovated and modernised.

The Railway Station

A view looking towards Leicester, taken in August 1959. The former Midland Railway tracks were to the right where the ex-Midlands locomotive No. 43261 is waiting on the up line. The former LNWR lines were to the left and crossed over the Midland at the bridge in the far distance. Immediately in front of the trains in the modern photograph the extension to the original platform is visible. The electrification of this route by 2015 will prompt major changes to this scene.

The Workhouse

The Market Harborough Union workhouse was erected to the north of the town and right on the town's boundary in 1836/37. The architect was Sampson Kempthorne, who designed many workhouses, but this was the only example of his work in this area. The site is now St Luke's Hospital and the new Day Case Unit is located close to where the original workhouse lodge stood. Some of the later workhouse buildings dating to the early twentieth century have survived.

The Congregational Chapel

A sedate building, set back from the bustle of the street, the chapel was built in 1844 at the northern end of High Street on the site of an earlier manse and designed by William Flint of Leicester. The Congregationalists had been active in the town since as early as the Act of Uniformity of 1662. A large hall was constructed behind the church in 1875. Both buildings are still in use. The famous Congregationalist minister and hymn writer Philip Doddridge is commemorated in the name of the nearby road. He was a student and the later head of the Dissenting Academy at Kibworth and in both Kibworth and Market Harborough from 1725 to 1729.

Welland Park, Rose Garden
The park has maintained its original Edwardian character to a remarkable degree. Following a period of municipal neglect, local government investment has restored the differing aspects of this delightful open space, including this formal rose garden.

Garden of Remembrance
A small oasis of peace, situated close to the Square and the centre of the town, this small garden has been renovated by the local council and a group of locally based charities.

CHAPTER 3

The Villages

Created as a place for trading, Market Harborough is still dependent upon the villages that cluster around it for its economic prosperity. Those who live in the countryside also look towards the town for local governance. Harborough District Council is the largest of the district authorities in Leicestershire and covers almost a quarter of the county, embracing eighty-five separate parishes.

Historically, the town was formerly an urban district. These authorities were formed in 1895, principally to address public health issues in urban areas, and were often based on the earlier poor law union boundaries. Under the Local Government Act of 1974 the Market Harborough Urban District Council was abolished and replaced by the larger Harborough District Council with its headquarters in the town. In many parts of the country, new parish councils were formed to provide local governance for small towns that had previously been urban districts, but this was not the case in Market Harborough which today is 'parish-less'.

In Saxon times the administrative power of this area was centred at Bowden. Its domination over the surrounding settlements probably stretched back to Edward the Confessor and it was still an ancient royal demesne in 1247. As late as 1605, James I confirmed the manorial tenants' immunity from subscribing to the maintenance of the knights of the shire while parliament was sitting, indicating that Bowden's ancient status was still recognised.

Connected to the town by the coaching route from Leicester to Northampton, the two Kibworth villages provided a resting place for travellers, particularly within the numerous coaching inns along the old Main Street in Kibworth Harcourt. Here, it was necessary for the coaches to negotiate many sharp bends and turns in the road and a steep incline in order to ford a brook. Accidents were frequent. One man, Michael Ingo, aged seventy-three years, was killed when an express coach overturned on the approach from Market Harborough around midnight on 21 April 1834. There is a slate to his memory in the churchyard.

It was here, close to where the Nonconformists of the Congregational church had their Dissenting Academy, that Thomas Cook, a dissenter of another persuasion, and a man who recognised the damaging effects of alcohol, socially and spiritually, had his dream of universal travel.

In June 1905 some 450 or more unemployed men from Leicester marched to London. One of their leaders was the Revd Frederic Donaldson of St Mark's, Leicester, known as the 'vicar of the unemployed'. On their long journey south, they were provided with sustenance and footwear by those who supported their campaign. On their return, on Sunday 18 June 1905, supporters on bicycles rode out from Leicester to greet than as they crossed the county boundary from Northamptonshire back into

Market Harborough. They followed the old turnpike and rested outside the parish church of St Wilfrid in Kibworth Beauchamp.

Harborough has been hunting country for centuries. The area south of the town was part of the old Rockingham Forest, a royal hunting forest from the time of William the Conqueror. Leicestershire is considered to be the birthplace of fox hunting in the form it is known today. The 'father' of English fox hunting, Hugo Meynell, rented Langton Hall and stayed in the area during the season. As with other Leicestershire market towns, hunting attracted wealthy visitors and participants who would stay at local manor houses, halls and hunting lodges, and many different trades and enterprises grew up to service their requirements including leather and footwear manufacturing, saddlers, blacksmiths, and veterinary practitioners. Some of these businesses are still evident in Market Harborough.

The villages of the Harborough area each have a distinctive character and a rich history. Medbourne has Roman origins, which are still to be explored. Nearby Hallaton is well-known for the remarkable Hallaton Hoard, discovered in 2000 by the village's own Fieldwork Group. Gumley was an important centre for the kings of Mercia who met here in AD 749. King Offa attended the Witan (or meeting of the wise men) here in 772 and 779

The first performance of the oratorio *Messiah* by George Frederick Handel took place at Church Langton in 1751, just months after the composer's death. William Hanbury, the rector of church Langton who instigated the event, recorded in his diary that the doors of the church were flung open so that everyone in the surrounding countryside could hear the music. In that time before rural modern noise pollution caused by road traffic, aircraft and railways, and when few people in the countryside had ever heard an organ being played, this must certainly have been a momentous and memorable experience. It was also a financial success. Hanbury records that there were no vacancies at any inn between the village and Market Harborough. Several miles away, in the churchyard at Burton Overy, is a tombstone, on which is engraved a line of music from the oratorio. It is suggested locally that the young man who lies buried beneath this memorial took part in that historic performance. The festival, which included other musical performances, drew such crowds to this quiet corner of Leicestershire that the convening stagecoaches totally jammed the village roads leading from the turnpike.

St Mary in Arden

This was the original parish church of Market Harborough, rebuilt in about 1693 to designs by Henry Dormer on the site of the earlier church. The present ruins retain some Norman decoration as well as the early fifteenth century outer doorway. The churchyard was the only burial ground for the people of Market Harborough until 1878 and some memorials are still standing, including some of local Swithland slate. However, many have been moved from their original positions during attempts at renovating and refurbishing the site.

Little Bowden, Old Rectory
This delightful house dates from 1627. Its soft yellowish stone is more common in villages south of here, and indeed Little Bowden was in Northamptonshire until boundary changes in 1891 and again in 1895.

Little Bowden, The Barn

An unusual name for a grand country house, but The Barn, overlooking Market Harborough, was designed in the late eighteenth century as a hunting lodge. The owner, Edward Kennard, also created a nine-hole golf course in around 1900. The house was destroyed by fire in 1912. Today, stylish but smaller residences line the original drive, which is named Shrewsbury Terrace after another former owner.

Little Bowden Parish Church

Little Bowden rejoined Leicestershire in 1888. Although Market Harborough has encroached, a distinct village atmosphere still prevails. The parish church of The Transfiguration: St Nicholas dates to the twelfth century. In recent years it has been extended to include a meeting room.

Great Bowden Parish Church

Great Bowden was a major Saxon settlement and the centre of a legislation that included twelve other villages. The parish church of St Peter and St Paul is mentioned in about 1220 in association with another chapel, which is assumed to be the church of St Mary in Arden.

Great Bowden Pond Green, 1907

People have been living here since the Iron Age. It became a divided settlement in the tenth century, when land on the southern side of the River Welland was acquired by Northamptonshire while the remaining land stayed within the Viking Danelaw. The village's fields once extended beyond the current parish boundaries and included much of what is now Market Harborough. The pond was filled in 1928.

Theddingworth Smeeton Institute

This neat building of considerable character is now the village hall. It was built in 1893 by a local man, John Smeeton, as a village recreation and reading room in memory of his son Percy, who died in 1889.

Lubbenham Village Pond

Originally, this area was known locally as the 'town pit'. It was a pond, and the walls around it date from 1869. This photograph was taken about forty years later. In 1919, the pond was filled in and a war memorial constructed above it. Some of the parapets of the nineteenth-century wall remain.

Foxton Main Street

The village of Foxton was changed forever when the canal was cut through, creating new roads and bridges. The natural rising landscape of Main Street up towards the church was enhanced to provide a bridge over the canal, which winds its way, eventually, to the Union Wharf at Market Harborough.

Gumley Hall

The hall was built in 1764 for Joseph Cradock, and demolished in 1964 having never recovered from its military occupation during the Second World War. It was once renowned for its fine library. The residents enjoyed a picturesque view across the countryside towards Northamptonshire framed by the trees that once lined the drive.

Gumley Hall Party

Gumley has a long and fascinating history. Here, King Aethelbald of Mercia held a synod in AD 749. Near to the site of the hall, and close to the parish church of St Helen, is a pond known as The Mot, which may be of Saxon origin, and it is known that King Offa attended the Witanagemot for the kings of Mercia here in 772 and 779.

North Kilworth Cottage

The white-painted, half timbered cottage is a modern design feature of so many villages, but this is original. Buildings often lose chimneys, but this cottage has gained one in the century between the two photographs.

South Kilworth

A fine example of a prosperous yeoman's house, dating from the mid-sixteenth century, located at the heart of the village, near to the village green and church. A building of extensive proportions, it was photographed in the 1940s by Frederick Attenborough.

Hallaton Butter Cross

The butter 'cross' is not a cross, but a cone shaped structure that has served as a meeting or moot point for the village for centuries. It has close associations with the ancient Easter Monday Bottle-kicking. The tradition of donating food to the poor is continued in a ceremony of giving penny loaves at the Butter Cross before the bottle-kicking contest begins.

Hallaton Manor House

An impressive building in the Tudor style, but constructed in 1845, it is said to incorporate stone from its predecessor, which was located in the centre of the village. After the Second World War, the house was owned for just three years by a Leicester antique dealer, who sold it to the Sundial Nursing Home. It continues to serve as a specialist residential home today.

Medbourne Church and Bridge
The bridge is said to date from the thirteenth century and is situated in the centre of this ancient village, but there may have been an even earlier crossing of the Medbourne Brook nearby on the line of the Roman Gartree Road. Less than 150 metres away, evidence of a Roman villa was discovered in 1721, and an elaborate mosaic pavement was recorded in excavations in 1877.

Medbourne Rectory

The Old Rectory, which stands in secluded gardens still surrounded by tall trees, dates mainly from around 1830 and may stand on the site of its medieval predecessor. It certainly contains elements of two earlier buildings from the seventeenth and eighteenth centuries. It was sold by the church in 1952 for £3,800 when a new and much smaller rectory was built in the paddock behind.

Medbourne, No. 3 Spring Bank

The older photograph dates to the 1930s when this picturesque shop accommodated the village grocer. Groceries are still sold here today, including cider from the local Bottle Kicking Cider Company, and it is also the post office at the centre of the local community.

Tur Langton Chequers Inn

At one time the small village of Tur Langton had three public houses. Only one now remains. The Chequers was situated on Main Street near the edge of the village. This earlier photograph was taken in around 1905.

Tur Langton Main Street
The tower spire of St Andrew's dominates the cottages on Main Street. Designed by Leicester architect Joseph Goddard, the church is an unusual but successful example of the Early English style, built in exposed brick in 1866.

West Langton Hall

Built in the early 1600s, West Langton Hall has seen many owners and occupiers. Hugo Meynell brought the Quorn hounds here in the 1770s to hunt south-east Leicestershire, and the antiquary Thomas Staveley, who died in 1684, was born here. A more recent owner was Robert Spencer, cousin to Princess Diana, who maintained a wild bird sanctuary in the grounds. Some claim the building is haunted: an alleged bloodstained floorboard is said never to dry out.

Church Langton Parish Church

It was here that the first performance in an English parish church of Handel's oratorio *Messiah* took place, part of a plan by the then rector William Hanbury to create a grand minster church in this quiet village. The Hanbury Foundation continues to fund local education to this day.

Kibworth Harcourt, the Rose & Crown

Perhaps Kibworth's best-known coaching inn, on the turnpike from Market Harborough to Leicester, the former Rose & Crown has been a landmark since the eighteenth century. In its heyday up to twenty coaches stopped here each day. The 'front' of the inn was originally the side elevation (on the left) facing Main Street.

Kibworth Harcourt, the White House
Standing on the Main Street, this is a building with a fascinating and somewhat mysterious history. It was the home of the famous Dissenting Academy of Revd John Jennings, who also instituted the nearby Congregational chapel. It was later The Crown, another coaching inn, and coaches would pull up in the yard at the back to offload their passengers and goods. It is also said that the house is haunted.

Kibworth Harcourt, the Old House

William Parker, whose family had lived in Kibworth for at least five generations, built the Old House in 1678. It was later acquired by an attorney, Thomas Peach, and may have been associated at some time with the nearby Dissenting Academy. In the twentieth century its most famous occupant was General Jack, a distinguished First World War soldier. A plaque was fixed to the building in 2013 commemorating other distinguished former occupants, the writer Anna Letitia Barbauld and her father, the Unitarian preacer John Aiken.

Kibworth Beauchamp, the Coach & Horses

The Whitsuntide Village Feast was held here at one time, and a member of my family, Henry Woodford, was the landlord in the late nineteenth century. The original inn dates to the seventeenth century. A long wooden horse trough stood in front of the inn for many years, in which local boys sometimes sailed paper boats and other items, and where sometimes a drunken brawler was ducked in order to cool off.

Kibworth Beauchamp, the Manor House

This lovely house may be one of only two H-shaped Elizabethan dwellings still surviving in the country. It dates to the late 1500s but has some eighteenth-century alterations. The older photograph was taken in the 1970s by the late Bert Aggas, a local archaeologist and historian.

Smeeton Westerby, the Old Forge

On the corner of Blacksmith's Lane, Smeeton's smithy closed in 1902 when Robert Smalley was the blacksmith. Next door was the village's first sub-post office.

St Michael and All Angels, Cranoe
The entire population of Cranoe could fit inside their parish church many times over. Once a thriving village, the school, the post office and the inn have all closed. All the village buildings and land except the church are owned by the Brudenell estate, to which the occupants still pay rent.

CHAPTER 4

Foxton Locks &
The Grand Union Canal

A walk through one of Market Harborough's modern industrial estates by the side of the River Welland could not be described as a picturesque experience. The buildings have been constructed for a specific purpose. They are uniform in design, lacking in character and devoid of charm. They house a variety of industries and manufacturing activities, which in some cases produce waste materials and noise. The processes being carried out also require raw materials, so there is a constant movement of vehicles, delivering, collecting, loading and unloading.

A similar industrial environment would have been the experience of any observer at Foxton Locks from the mid-nineteenth century. Set in the gentle, undulating green landscape of south Leicestershire, the towpaths now provide pleasant walks for hikers and holidaymakers, and the long repetitive process of raising the colourful narrowboats up and down the staircase of locks is a fascinating distraction to which adjectives such as 'picturesque' and 'quant' are often applied.

But when the Grand Union Canal came to this countryside, life changed dramatically for the inhabitants of the nearby villages such as Foxton and Gumley. Armies of 'navvies' lived here for the duration of the construction, setting up their own communities and bringing their own way of life to the insular settlements. The canals were engineering projects on a massive scale, requiring the excavation of embankments and the movement of vast amounts of materials.

Then, in the early years of the twentieth century, the builders returned, this time with machinery, to construct the inclined plane by the side of the locks. All day, the local people would have heard the sound of the steam engine that moved the caissons that lifted the canal boats slowly up and down the incline. Six thousand tons of cargo could be shifted between the two levels in one twelve-hour day. Such engineering required constant maintenance, night and day.

Historically, every new innovation results in the decline of a previous industry. The old staircase of narrow locks became neglected and fell into disrepair. But the inclined plane at Foxton was successful for only a relatively short period of time. There were design problems, such as the wear on the tracks caused by the weight of the caissons. Less than thirty years after this massive structure had been built, it was shut down and largely dismantled. The locks were refurbished, but the canals were no longer the principal means of moving goods across the country. The railways were now extending their reach into every town and city in England and beyond. No less than five routes converged on Market Harborough, causing a major downturn in business on both roads and the canals.

Today the canal network is becoming a major tourist and holiday attraction, but also an important ecological environment where wildlife and wildflowers can thrive and be protected.

Foxton Locks
The location within the countryside of south Leicestershire provides an air of tranquillity to what is really an industrial scene that changed the landscape dramatically. Substantial investment in recent years has created a top national tourist attraction.

Inclined Plane

The inclined plane was constructed in 1900 to relieve the congestion of boats waiting to pass through the two sets of ten locks, and to allow wider boats to use the system. Powered by a stationary steam engine, two boats could be moved in twelve minutes. Plans are in hand to restore the plane to working condition.

The Grand Union Canal, Market Harborough Section
This short branch of the canal system connecting Foxton Locks with Market Harborough ends in what is now an attractive and developing North Wharf, combining residential areas with facilities for narrowboats.

The Locks Staircase
Completed in 1814, Foxton Locks is the largest flight of staircase locks on the English canal system. It takes seventy-five minutes for a boat to move through the flight.

Acknowledgements

The Harborough Mail, with particular thanks to the editor. Alex Blackwell, for allowing me full access to the paper's remarkable archives.

Dr Ben Brooksbank.

Flight Lieutenant John Standish MBE, 1084 Squadron (Market Harborough) Air Training Corps.